To Be an Artist

Maya Ajmera & John D. Ivanko

Foreword by Jacques d'Amboise

A GLOBAL FUND FOR
Children
BOOK

Charlesbridge

Mexico

The Artist and a Sense of Wonder

Have you ever thought of what a wonderful word "wonder" is? It describes the heart and mind filled with amazement: Oh, I'm so happy; I feel wonderful. It expresses curiosity about the world: I wonder what makes fire hot? I wonder what's out there on the other side of the stars? It expresses our inner thoughts: I wonder what she is thinking? I wonder if he likes me?

Wonder is generated from the grand in size— the stars, galaxies, and universe—to the tiny—the molecules, atoms, and particles. Wonder comes from the experiences of your life, your consciousness, and the relationships you make with other people. All individuals are evolving and wondering, creating the story chapters of their lives moment by moment— just as you are, even as you read this book. Wow! What a wonderful miracle is the human being!

How do we humans best express these feelings and the sense of wonder that comes out of us? We make art. We invented it: music, dance, drawing, painting, sculpting, architecture, drama, storytelling, poetry, song, and literature. These arts touch and change our lives, opening up our hearts and minds to all kinds of possibilities. Every time you use art to communicate, you become an artist, expressing the wonders of being human.

—JACQUES D'AMBOISE

FORMER PRINCIPAL DANCER OF THE NEW YORK CITY BALLET

FOUNDER OF THE NATIONAL DANCE INSTITUTE

To be an artist means expressing yourself in many different ways.

France

Tanzania

Art can be just about anything. Painting, singing, dancing, playing music, and writing poetry are popular forms of art around the world. But so are acting in a play, telling a story, weaving a basket, or making a sculpture out of clay. Dressing up, making sandcastles, taking a photograph . . . these are all ways you can show your creativity.

China

Colombia

United States

To be an artist means drawing and designing . . .

Japan

Iraq

France

Vietnam

There are lots of ways to make a picture. You can use paint, pencils, crayons, chalk, or markers. You can start from scratch or color in an outline. The thoughts and feelings you have and the way you combine your subject, colors, and textures are what make your pictures works of art.

. . . and coloring and painting.

India

United States

South Africa

Ukraine

Playing with colors is a lot of fun. With a swirl of a brush, you can mix blue and red paint to make purple, or mix yellow and red to make orange.

You can paint almost anything anywhere—on a canvas, a wall, or even an egg.

Ecuador

To be an artist means
making music—
playing drums of all
shapes and sizes . . .

Indonesia

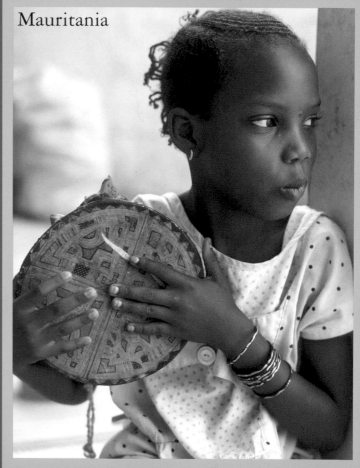

Mauritania

India

United States

Jamaica

Music is fun to listen to, dance to, sing, and play. It can be happy or sad, slow or fast. Anyone can be a musician. You can play all kinds of musical instruments.

. . .or blowing on horns and flutes. . .

United States

Finland

Indonesia

Peru

They can be big, like a tuba, or small, like a kazoo. You can even use your own body as an instrument to sing, hum, tap, and whistle.

Germany

Bhutan

. . . playing with little strings or big strings . . .

China

India

Slovak Republic

United States

Spain

Whether they like to sing, play, or listen, people all over the world like to get into the rhythm of music.

. . . or singing songs.

Japan

United States

Singing is popular around the world. You may sing songs at school or in a rock band. Others may sing a hymn in a church choir. But sometimes, it is just fun to sing in the shower or while taking a walk.

Sweden

United States

To be an artist means dancing your favorite steps and moves . . .

All over the world, people dance at celebrations, on stage, or while listening to the radio. You can dance by yourself, with friends, with a partner, or in a group. Moving your body to music allows you to have fun and let your feelings out. Some dances have special steps.

United States

Cuba

Eritrea

Cambodia

Spain

Austria

Japan

. . . or performing traditional dances at festivals.

Canada

Mexico

Many cultures have traditional dances to celebrate special occasions. You may wear colorful dresses or costumes and have certain steps that reflect the meaning of the dance. Other dances you can make up as you go along.

Federated States of Micronesia

To be an artist means writing a poem or story . . .

Pakistan

Bolivia

Nigeria

You can express many things with words. Poems, stories, and plays are all forms of art. Your poem or story can be published in a magazine or made into a book. Your play can be performed by actors on stage.

United States

Philippines

. . . or acting in a play.

You are an actor or thespian when you perform in a play or movie. Before the opening show, you have to rehearse your lines for many days. You may also wear a special costume to become a certain character.

India

To be an artist means
sculpting a work of art,

United States

Tanzania

weaving a basket or
colorful cloth . . .

United States

Bhutan

Using clay, you can sculpt a bowl or an animal. With sand, you can create a castle. You can chisel a piece of rock to make jewelry. Kids weave to make colorful cloth or baskets out of leaves. Sewing different patterns on to a cloth is called embroidery. With all these forms of art, you use your fingers and hands in intricate ways.

Mexico

. . . or stitching a unique pattern.

To be an artist means sharing your artistic flair . . .

South Africa

United States

India

Bulgaria

artist in . . .

Iraq

Germany

Nigeria

Bhutan

United States

Sweden

To Be an Artist is dedicated to Life Pieces to Masterpieces of Washington, D.C. —M. A.

For the "seventh generation of children on earth."—J. D. I.

To Be an Artist was developed by the Global Fund for Children, a nonprofit organization committed to advancing the dignity of children and youth around the world. Global Fund for Children books teach young people to value diversity and help them become productive and caring global citizens. Visit www.lifepieces.org to learn more about Life Pieces to Masterpieces, a grantee partner of the Global Fund for Children (www.globalfundforchildren.org).

Developed by Global Fund for Children Books
1101 Fourteenth Street, NW, Suite 420
Washington, DC 20005
(202) 331-9003 • www.globalfundforchildren.org

Published by Charlesbridge
85 Main Street
Watertown, MA 02472
(617) 926-0329
www.charlesbridge.com

Details about the donation of royalties can be obtained by writing to Charlesbridge Publishing and the Global Fund for Children.

Library of Congress Cataloging-in-Publication Data
Ajmera, Maya.
  To be an artist / Maya Ajmera, John D. Ivanko ; editor, Yolanda LeRoy.
    p. cm.
  Summary: An introduction to using various art forms to express creativity.
  ISBN 978-1-57091-503-1 (reinforced for library use)
  ISBN 978-1-57091-576-5 (softcover)
  1. Arts—Juvenile literature. [1. Arts. 2. Creative ability.] I. Ivanko, John D. (John Duane), 1966– II. LeRoy, Yolanda. III. Title.
NX633.A36 2004 700—dc21   2003008154

Printed in Korea
(hc) 10 9 8 7 6 5
(sc) 10 9 8

Display type and text type set in Garamond No. 3
Color separated by Sung In Printing
Printed December 2013 by Sung In Printing in Gunpo-Si, Kyonggi-Do, Korea
Production supervision by Brian G. Walker and Linda Jackson
Designed by Susan Mallory Sherman

As always, my deepest thanks to John Ivanko for his constant support and creativity. Thank you to Joan Shifrin and Kelly Swanson Turner of the Global Fund for Children for their support as well.
    —Maya Ajmera

I wish to thank my ever-cheering wife, Lisa Kivirst, and my son, Liam Ivanko Kivirst, who let me take a break from playing together to complete this book. It has been such a wonderful creative partnership to work with Maya Ajmera and to share in her vision of what the world can become, one child at a time.
    —John Ivanko

Our thanks to all the photographers who participated in this project. Without the photographs, there would be no book. Many thanks also to Jacques d'Amboise and Elle Hauck of the National Dance Institute. Financial support for this project has been provided by the Flora Family Foundation, W. K. Kellogg Foundation, and generous individual donors.